Kobe Bryant

Additional Titles in the Sports Reports *Series*

Roberto Alomar
Star Second Baseman
(0-7660-1079-1)

Charles Barkley
Star Forward
(0-89490-655-0)

Mark Brunell
Star Quarterback
(0-7660-1830-X)

Kobe Bryant
Star Guard
(0-7660-1828-8)

Terrell Davis
Star Running Back
(0-7660-1331-6)

Tim Duncan
Star Forward
(0-7660-1334-0)

Dale Earnhardt
Star Race Car Driver
(0-7660-1335-9)

Brett Favre
Star Quarterback
(0-7660-1332-4)

Kevin Garnett
Star Forward
(0-7660-1829-6)

Jeff Gordon
Star Race Car Driver
(0-7660-1083-X)

Wayne Gretzky
Star Center
(0-89490-930-4)

Ken Griffey, Jr.
Star Outfielder
(0-89490-802-2)

Scott Hamilton
Star Figure Skater
(0-7660-1236-0)

Anfernee Hardaway
Star Guard
(0-7660-1234-4)

Tim Hardaway
Star Guard
(0-7660-1500-9)

Grant Hill
Star Forward
(0-7660-1078-3)

Allen Iverson
Star Guard
(0-7660-1501-7)

Michael Jordan
Star Guard
(0-89490-482-5)

Shawn Kemp
Star Forward
(0-89490-929-0)

Jason Kidd
Star Guard
(0-7660-1333-2)

Michelle Kwan
Star Figure Skater
(0-7660-1504-1)

Tara Lipinski
Star Figure Skater
(0-7660-1505-X)

Mark Messier
Star Center
(0-89490-801-4)

Reggie Miller
Star Guard
(0-7660-1082-1)

Randy Moss
Star Wide Receiver
(0-7660-1504-1)

Chris Mullin
Star Forward
(0-89490-486-8)

Hakeem Olajuwon
Star Center
(0-89490-803-0)

Shaquille O'Neal
Star Center
(0-89490-656-9)

Gary Payton
Star Guard
(0-7660-1330-8)

Scottie Pippen
Star Forward
(0-7660-1080-5)

Jerry Rice
Star Wide Receiver
(0-89490-928-2)

Cal Ripken, Jr.
Star Shortstop
(0-89490-485-X)

David Robinson
Star Center
(0-89490-483-3)

Barry Sanders
Star Running Back
(0-89490-484-1)

Deion Sanders
Star Athlete
(0-89490-652-6)

Junior Seau
Star Linebacker
(0-89490-800-6)

Emmitt Smith
Star Running Back
(0-89490-653-4)

Frank Thomas
Star First Baseman
(0-89490-659-3)

Chris Webber
Star Forward
(0-89490-799-9)

Tiger Woods
Star Golfer
(0-7660-1081-3)

SPORTS REPORTS

Kobe Bryant

Star Guard

Nick Kennedy

ROCK FALLS
H.S. LIB.

Enslow Publishers, Inc.
40 Industrial Road   PO Box 38
Box 398   Aldershot
Berkeley Heights, NJ 07922   Hants GU12 6BP
USA   UK
http://www.enslow.com

Copyright © 2002 by Nick Kennedy

All rights reserved.

No part of this book may be reproduced by any means without the written permission of the publisher.

Library of Congress Cataloging-in-Publication Data

Kennedy, Nick.
  Kobe Bryant : star guard / Nick Kennedy.
     p. cm. — (Sports reports))
  Includes bibliographical references (p.) and index.
  Summary: Looks at the personal life and professional basketball career of NBA star Kobe Bryant of the Los Angeles Lakers.
  ISBN 0-7660-1828-8
  1. Bryant, Kobe, 1978—Juvenile literature. 2. Basketball players—United States—Biography—Juvenile literature. [1. Bryant, Kobe, 1978- 2. Basketball players. 3. African Americans—Biography.] I. Title. II. Series.
  GV884.B794 K46   2002b
  796.323'092—dc211
                                                                   2001007049

Printed in the United States of America

10 9 8 7 6 5 4 3 2

To Our Readers:
We have done our best to make sure that all Internet Addresses in this book were active and appropriate when we went to press. However, the author and publisher have no control over and assume no liability for the material available on those Internet sites or on other Web sites they may link to. Any comments or suggestions can be sent by e-mail to comments@enslow.com or to the address on the back cover.

Photo Credits: © Allsport, pp. 14, 16, 54, 60, 72, 80, 91; Courtesy of Connie Egan, pp. 22, 24, 27, 31, 34, 37, 38, 40, 45, 47, 87; Courtesy of Nick Kennedy, p. 50.

Cover Photo: © Allsport

Contents

1 A Star Is Born. 7

2 Childhood 19

3 State Champ 29

4 Joining the Lakers 43

5 All-Star Player 57

6 Welcome Dennis Rodman 65

7 The Champs! 74

8 Kobe off the Court 86

9 The 2000–2001 Season 89

Chapter Notes. 93

Career Statistics. 99

Where to Write and
Internet Addresses. 101

Index. 103

Acknowledgments

Special thanks go to Connie and Michael Egan for their assistance in writing this book.

Chapter 1

A Star Is Born

Only a handful of athletes have dominated a team sport as thoroughly as Michael Jordan did in the 1990s. He led the Chicago Bulls to six National Basketball Association (NBA) titles. He was named the Most Valuable Player in all six title runs.

So, as Jordan began to think about retiring, basketball fans began wondering who would be the next Air Jordan. Many players auditioned for the role. Grant Hill, the Duke University star, came into the NBA and made an instant splash with the Detroit Pistons. Jerry Stackhouse, who attended Jordan's University of North Carolina, seemed a possibility when the Philadelphia 76ers drafted him in 1995. One player, the University of Southern California's Harold Minor, reminded people so much of his Airness that he even earned the nickname "Baby Jordan."

In 1996, while Jordan was leading the Bulls to the first title of their second "three-peat," a skinny high school kid in Ardmore, Pennsylvania, was also auditioning for his job. His name was Kobe Bryant.

Bryant accomplished much in his senior year in high school. He was named *USA Today's* National High School Player of the Year. He also led his team to the Pennsylvania State Championship. Talk of his plans after high school centered on whether he would join Coach Mike Krzyzewski (sha-chef-ski) at Duke University or Rick Pitino at Kentucky. Although he was criticized at the time, Bryant decided to skip college altogether and go directly into the NBA from high school.

He ended up with the Los Angeles Lakers, and he made an immediate impact in his first year in the league. He became the youngest first-year player ever to start in an NBA game. In his second year, the fans voted him the youngest All-Star in NBA history.

Bryant and teammate Shaquille O'Neal made

the Lakers a team to be reckoned with. They made the playoffs in each of Bryant's first three years. In 1998, they even made it to the Western Conference Finals.

Kobe Bryant continued to improve his game each year. He set personal records in points per game and rebounds per game. But as the 1999–2000 season began, he and the Lakers still had not won an NBA championship. Without one, Bryant would not be considered the true successor to Michael Jordan. To help him get there, the Lakers hired Phil Jackson as their coach. Jackson had been Michael Jordan's coach with the Bulls.

The Lakers finished the 1999–2000 season with the best record in the Western Conference. They started their playoff journey with a series against the Sacramento Kings. The Lakers struggled through all five games before eliminating the Kings. Some people began to wonder if the Lakers had what it took to win the championship.

But the Lakers went on to beat the Phoenix Suns in five games. Next up, the Western Conference Finals against the Portland Trail Blazers. The Blazers were set to give the Lakers a real battle. Big, strong players dominated their lineup.

The Lakers shot out to a three games to one lead in the series. They had a chance to finish off the Trail Blazers at home, but Portland battled back. Behind Scottie Pippen and all-star Rasheed Wallace, the Blazers came back and tied the series at three games apiece. In Game 7, the Trail Blazers were actually on the verge of stunning the Lakers. They had a 16-point lead in the fourth quarter.

But Kobe Bryant and Shaquille O'Neal led their team back. Their defense dug in and caused the Trail Blazers to miss 14 of their last 15 shots. The Lakers won the game. It was on to the NBA Finals for Kobe Bryant and the Los Angeles Lakers. The team would be playing Reggie Miller and the Indiana Pacers. After the game, Bryant talked about the importance of his team's effort.

"This was the ultimate test to this point," Bryant said. "They had us down 13 going into the fourth quarter. This was a huge challenge for us."[1]

In the Finals against the Pacers, the Lakers led the series 1–0 and were in control in Game 2 when they suffered a major blow. Bryant went up for a jump shot. As he came down, his left foot landed on a defender's foot. He grabbed his ankle and twisted on the floor in pain while the game continued.

When the referees finally blew their whistles, the Lakers' trainers ran out onto the court to attend to Bryant. He managed to get up, but he could barely walk. He went to the locker room and the game resumed.

The television announcers reported that Bryant's ankle had been X-rayed, and his foot was not broken. Reports said that Bryant might even come back into the game. The Lakers pulled away from the Pacers and won the game. But Bryant would not be back. After the game, it was apparent that his sprain was worse than expected. He needed crutches to walk. He would not be able to play in the third game of the series.

The Lakers missed Kobe Bryant. Without him in the lineup and the series switching back to Indiana, the Pacers played with confidence. They cut the Lakers' series lead to two games to one with a 100–91 win.

On Wednesday, June 14, 2000, the Pacers were looking to tie the series. Bryant had been through many hours of therapy for his sprained ankle. But he was still not completely healthy. Reporters wanted to know if there was a possibility the injury might cause him to miss this crucial Finals game. "I don't think so," said Bryant.[2]

Kobe Bryant was determined to play. But

FACT

In 1895, Wilhelm Conrad Roentgen discovered radiation that could penetrate matter where visible light could not. He called this radiation X-rays. The "X" stood for unknown. X-rays help doctors look for injuries inside people's bodies without having to operate on them.

would he be at his best? The injury would hurt his ability to play defense, cut to the basket on offense, and jump for rebounds.

"I have all summer to rest it," said Bryant. "This is the end of the season right here, so I'm not really concerned about re-injuring my ankle."[3]

The Pacers started off the game playing with the confidence they showed in Game 3. Bryant was wincing as he moved on his sore ankle. He struggled to keep up with Indiana guard Mark Jackson.

The pressure grew in the second half. At one point, the Lakers were up by five points. Then the Pacers went on a 12–2 run that gave them a five-point lead.

"We'd score, they'd come back and score, we'd score, they'd score. You could get mad because our defense was lacking, but at the same time it was fun," Bryant said after the game. "This is the type of thing you watch growing up—the ultimate, the NBA Finals."[4]

The game ended in a tie score, 104–104. The two teams would have to play a five-minute overtime period.

The Lakers started strongly in overtime, taking a 110–106 lead. But with only 2:33 left, the unthinkable happened. MVP Lakers center

Shaquille O'Neal went for a rebound over the back of Pacers center Rick Smits. O'Neal was called for his sixth foul, and was out of the game. The Lakers would have to do it without Shaq. That is when Kobe Bryant stepped up.

First he launched a twenty-three-foot jump shot over the outstretched arm of Reggie Miller from the top of the key. The ball hit nothing but net and the Lakers went up, 114–111.

The Pacers tried to take advantage of Shaq's absence. They went to their seven-foot four-inch center, Rick Smits, who nailed a short jump-hook shot. Then Bryant hit another long jump shot with Mark Jackson's hand in his face. That put the Lakers back up by three. "I just relaxed like I was playing in the back yard," Bryant said later.[5]

The game was coming down to the final seconds. Rick Smits made two shots from the foul line. Again the Pacers were within a point. Both teams were focused on the moment. The crowd in Indiana's Conseco Fieldhouse rose to its feet. The Lakers brought the ball up the court. If they turned the ball over or missed a shot, Indiana would have a chance to win the game.

Lakers guard Brian Shaw controlled the ball as the shot clock was winding down. He drove past a Pacers defender and launched an open shot in

Kobe Bryant takes it to the hoop against Indiana Pacers defender Austin Croshere during the 2000 NBA Finals.

the lane. Clang. The ball bounced high off the rim. Then it skimmed the backboard. The big men for the Lakers and Pacers all battled for position as they waited for the ball to come down.

But Kobe Bryant did not wait. He swooped in from the other side of the backboard, leaped in the air, grabbed the ball with both hands, and put the ball through the hoop for a reverse lay-up.

The Lakers bench went wild. Indiana fans were stunned. There were only 5.9 seconds left in the game. The Pacers still had a chance.

Indiana coach Larry Bird designed a play to go for the win. Reggie Miller was open for a three-point shot. He caught the inbounds pass. As Robert Horry flew at him, he launched a shot.

The ball bounced high off the rim—so high it went over the backboard. The horn sounded to end the game. The Lakers had won. Shaquille O'Neal and Kobe Bryant embraced on the court.

"This is the game I've been dreaming about, to be honest with you," Kobe said. "I dream about it every day."[6]

Teammate Glen Rice said it best. Speaking about Kobe Bryant, he said: "That was big-time tonight. That had to be the biggest performance since I've been watching and playing with him, of

Bryant leaps into the arms of teammate Shaquille O'Neal after the Lakers defeat the Pacers to win the 2000 NBA Championship.

his career. He stepped up like a veteran. That just goes to show how much he's matured."⁷

The Lakers went on to win the NBA Championship. Kobe Bryant had established himself as a superstar. Some of the greatest players that played the game were now praising this young star. "Pretty good for a 21-year-old," said Jerry West, a Hall-of-Famer who brought Bryant to the Lakers. "One of the happiest days of my life was when I thought we got the best player in the draft at No. 13. What's unique is he's only scratched the surface. Shaq is the scariest force I've seen in basketball, but if somebody ran their offense through Kobe, he'd be the scariest."⁸

Another Lakers great, Magic Johnson, had watched the game on television from his home in Los Angeles. His phone started to ring after the game ended. "Everybody called me," he said. "All the former players called and said, 'Man, now that is a superstar right there.' That was a career-defining game for him, without question. Everybody was searching for the guy, and with that performance he has become 'The Man.' He's ready to assume the role Michael had."⁹

With his performance in the 2000 NBA Finals, there was no question that Kobe Bryant had earned the high praise he was receiving. But when he made the jump from high school to the NBA, few people would have predicted that he would become a superstar so quickly. Few people knew how hard he worked, how dedicated he was, and how mature he was at such an early age.

The only thing people really knew about him, was that he came from a basketball family.

Chapter 2
Childhood

Joe "Jellybean" Bryant is Kobe's father. Very early in his basketball career, Joe Bryant earned a reputation as a "defensive specialist." At LaSalle University in Philadelphia, Bryant often used his quick hands and feet and his six-foot nine-inch frame to frustrate opposing players. Bryant left LaSalle in 1975, after his junior year, to play in the NBA. He was drafted by the Golden State Warriors but was then quickly traded to the Philadelphia 76ers. The highlight of Bryant's eight-year career occurred in 1977. That year, he played with Hall-of-Famer Julius Erving. Together, they helped the 76ers win the NBA's Eastern Conference Title.

Unfortunately, the 76ers lost in the NBA Finals to the Portland Trail Blazers. It was the closest Jellybean would come to acquiring his own NBA championship ring. On August 23 of the next year, Bryant was given another reason to celebrate. His wife, Pam, gave birth to their first son.

When Joe played in Philadelphia, he and Pam liked to eat at a Japanese steakhouse in King of Prussia, Pennsylvania. The Bryants named their new son after a type of steak on the menu at that restaurant—Kobe.

Kobe Bryant was three years old when he first showed an interest in basketball. His uncle Chubby Cox (a basketball star at Villanova University) gave him a toy Dr. J basketball rim. Kobe would set it up in front of the television and dunk the ball through the hoop while he watched his father play for the Clippers. His mother tried coaching him.

"I said, 'Sweetheart, you'll break it. Don't dunk. Just shoot jump shots and lay-ups.' The whole time they were on TV he would play too. He'd have his little cup of Gatorade and his towel and he'd say, 'Mom, I'm sweating.' Everything he does, he puts his heart into."[1]

Joe Bryant ended his NBA career in 1984. But he was not completely ready to give up basketball. At

FACT

Joe Bryant earned the nickname "Jellybean" because of the bright, fashionable clothes he wore. They were the same color as different flavors of jellybeans. His last coach in the NBA was Del Harris. Harris coached him when he played for the San Diego Clippers. Del Harris would also end up being Kobe's first NBA coach when he signed with the Los Angeles Lakers.

that time, the sport was growing more popular all around the world. Professional leagues had started in Europe. Many players with NBA experience were being recruited to play for European teams. Joe Bryant saw many benefits to living and working in Europe. He and his family would get to travel, live among a different culture, and possibly learn a new language.

He moved his wife, Kobe, and Kobe's older sisters, Shaya and Sharia, to Rieti, Italy. Although basketball was winning many new fans in Europe, soccer was still the number one sport in countries like Italy. "After school I would be the only guy on the basketball court, working on my moves, and then kids would start showing up with their soccer ball," Bryant said about playing basketball in Italy. "I could hold them off if there were two or three of them, but when they got to be eleven or twelve, I had to give up the court. It was either go home or be the goalkeeper."[2]

When he was not working on his moves at the playground, Kobe was going to school, learning to speak Italian, enjoying hikes in the mountains with his family, and attending basketball practice with his father. Kobe would work on his shot at an empty rim while his father's team played at the other end. With so

FACT

Rieti is a town in the center of Italy. It lies just to the north and west of Rome. Rome is the capital of Italy. Thousands of tourist flock to Italy every year to see such sights as the Roman Coliseum, the Sistine Chapel, and the Leaning Tower of Pisa. Italians have contributed much to the world in the areas of art, food, music, and literature.

Kobe Bryant's parents, Pam and Joe Bryant.

much going on in his young life, Kobe began to focus on what would become his real gift.

"Sure, we were in Italy, but he was around basketball all the time, playing against older guys," Joe Bryant said. "He was always wanting to play my teammates, and, you know, the older guys, they would pretend that they were falling down."[3]

Kobe's grandparents back in the United States also helped with his basketball education. They videotaped NBA games on television and sent them to Kobe in Europe. One of Kobe's first heroes was Los Angeles Lakers star guard Magic Johnson. Kobe would watch Magic's games over and over again. With his father's input, he would try to pick up the basics of the game. Kobe's enthusiasm, his confidence, and his strong work ethic were qualities that really emerged in those years.

The Bryants spent eight years in Europe. But in 1991, while Joe was playing for a team in Mulhouse, France, he decided it was time to go home. Although they had greatly enjoyed their experience in Europe, Joe and Pam knew it was time to think about their children's educational needs. They moved back to the Philadelphia area.

Kobe Bryant was in eighth grade at the time.

Kobe poses with his sisters, Shaya and Sharia.

Many kids his age had the advantage of playing in youth leagues and being schooled by coaches with years of basketball experience. Kobe had been in Europe for so long, he did not even know current American slang. Nobody knew who he was. But it did not take long for him to make a name for himself.

Philadelphia basketball legend Sonny Hill ran one of the more famous summer leagues in the area. When Kobe was filling out his application for the league, he was asked about his career plans. He wrote "NBA." A camp counselor tried to tell him that very few players ever make it to the NBA. But Kobe was determined.

"The guy said NBA players are one in a million," Bryant later recalled. "I said, 'Man, look, I'm going to be that one in a million.' You see Magic, Michael—they made it. What's different about them?"[4]

One coach who did not doubt Kobe Bryant's potential was Gregg Downer. Downer was the head basketball coach at Lower Merion High School in Ardmore, Pennsylvania. He was always watching players in middle school and grammar school. His job was to figure out how talented they were. He watched Kobe play in pick-up games at a local recreation center. Kobe dribbled well and rarely turned the ball over. Although he had skinny arms and legs, he was hitting more shots from the outside than most kids his age.

"When I first met him, at age 13, and I saw him play, after five minutes I said, 'This kid is going to be a pro,'" Downer said. "Never was there one moment I doubted that. That it would happen so quickly, I may have doubted that. But I knew if he progressed so quickly and continued to make good decisions, he would someday get there."[5]

Although Kobe Bryant had developed the basic elements of his game from watching the videotapes in Europe, he developed his unique style and one-on-one skills by playing against the better schoolyard players in the United States.

But the teacher who ultimately had the most impact on Kobe was his father. Joe Bryant talked to Kobe about the different aspects of the game. He also showed him how it was done.

Kobe Bryant started playing against his father in one-on-one games at an early age. But he did not start to beat him until he was sixteen. The games they played were physical. The two would throw elbows. Sometimes Kobe would end up with a bloody lip. "Then my mother would walk

Kobe (left) in the locker room with his high school coach Gregg Downer (right) and a friend.

out on the court, and the elbows would stop," Kobe said.[6]

Bryant soaked up all the basketball knowledge he could and tried to make himself a better player. When it was time to play basketball in high school, he was ready.

Chapter 3

State Champ

Basketball has continued to grow in popularity over the years in the United States. Many prep schools and private academies around the country have become very competitive. They have built strong basketball traditions by recruiting the best young players from their area. In the city of Philadelphia, the Philadelphia public and Catholic leagues have produced many top college and even some NBA stars. Many of these schools would have loved to have Kobe Bryant play for them.

But Joe Bryant did not want any special pressure on his son at an early age. When he graduated from the Bala Cynwyd Middle School,

Kobe enrolled in Lower Merion High School. Lower Merion had never been a basketball powerhouse. Like many high schools in the suburbs, lacrosse and soccer were more popular than basketball. When Gregg Downer took the coaching job, his goal was to make the Aces more competitive in the Central League. He wanted to compete with rivals Conestoga and Ridley. But when Kobe Bryant walked onto the court at Lower Merion, Downer rewrote his goals. He knew Kobe was special.

"I know the high school market very well and I've watched it for close to 20 years, and to think there could be another player come into my hands and be this good, that's an abstract concept," Downer said. "He's blessed with a lot of natural ability and great genes, but the work ethic is his and it's very strong. Kobe has the skills and the maturity and everything you could want."[1]

Kobe Bryant made an impact right away. With his skinny frame and baggy shorts, he did not look ready for the varsity team yet. But, in his freshman year, he led the team in scoring with 18 points per game. The Aces only won 4 games that year. But there was reason for optimism. The quick moves to the basket and the soft touch from

Kobe Bryant celebrates after a victory with his high school coaches and teammates.

the outside that Kobe had developed in Italy were starting to emerge in the Lower Merion gym.

He had grown to six feet five inches tall by his sophomore year, and he began to play all the positions on the court. He could bring the ball up on offense and box out the opponents' bigger players on defense. He averaged 22 points and 10 rebounds that year. He also led Lower Merion to the state playoffs where they eventually lost in the second round.

Kobe Bryant was impressive on the court. But basketball is a team game. Bryant's talents won a lot of games for his team. But to go far in the playoffs, he would need a supporting cast. An important piece to that puzzle was added during his junior year, when a freshman soccer player named Dan Pangrazio came along. Lower Merion's assistant basketball coach, Michael Egan, later described Pangrazio's introduction to Kobe Bryant. "Pangrazio was only a freshman but he was a pretty big kid and a good athlete. During his first practice, he drove into the lane and Kobe swatted his shot. The next time down the court, Pangrazio drove again and the same thing happened. Dan tried it one more time and Kobe swatted his shot again and let him know that freshmen don't come inside on him. That's when [he] decided to become a three-point shooter."[2]

With Kobe Bryant's talents emerging, Lower Merion was able to schedule more prominent opponents outside of the Central League. Early in the 1994–95 season, the Aces traveled to Jersey City, New Jersey, to take on St. Anthony's High School. St. Anthony's was coached by Bobby Hurley Sr. (father of point guard Bobby Hurley Jr.). Coach Hurley's talented team swarmed all over Kobe Bryant and the Aces.

But those tough early games paid off for Lower Merion. They beat arch-rival Ridley for the first time in years. Then they went on to capture the Central League crown. They finished with a 26–5 win-loss record and went into the postseason with great confidence.

In high school basketball in Pennsylvania, before the state playoffs begin, teams must first have a playoff for the district. Lower Merion was in District I. With Kobe Bryant's guidance they made it to the District Finals. The team they met there was Chester High School. The game was played at Villanova University's Dupont Pavilion.

Kobe Bryant's fame was spreading quickly. The week before the Chester game, his face appeared on the front page of a local weekly

Kobe in the Pennsylvania State High School Playoffs.

newspaper. Many Lower Merion fans brought the paper to the game and waved it. The Chester fans were not impressed. They mocked Bryant and their team ran all over the Aces. Despite a solid effort from Bryant and the rest of the team, Chester won the game, 77–50.

Despite the loss to Chester, Lower Merion qualified for the state playoffs. Their season came to a close with a loss to Hazleton High School. Kobe scored 33 points and added 15 rebounds in that game.

For most high school students, their senior year is a year for making decisions. Many choose to go on to college. Finding the right school can take a lot of work. Kobe Bryant would also have to make a decision by the end of the school year in 1995. But first he had to attend to some unfinished business.

After an impressive regular season, Lower Merion went into the state playoffs as the number one ranked team in Pennsylvania. Early in the tournament, they took on a talented, well-coached team from Cedar Cliff, Pennsylvania. Cedar Cliff was not intimidated. They ran sharp offensive plays and took an early lead over the Aces. They led by as many as eight points in the first half. Cedar Cliff fans sat behind the Lower Merion bench. They started to taunt the Aces. Gregg Downer knew it was time to make better use of Kobe Bryant's talents.

Coach Downer called for an alley-oop pass to Kobe. A Lower Merion guard lobbed the ball from the top of the key. But his pass was way too high, and it headed out of bounds.

"Kobe leaped way into the air and caught it with his left hand," Michael Egan said. "We were all excited because he was going to keep it from going out of bounds. But Kobe was able to swing his arm down and slam in through the rim. The play worked."³

Lower Merion went on a 12–0 run after that, and won the game to advance in the playoffs.

"After the game, all the coaches agreed that it was the best dunk we had see on any level," Egan said.⁴

To make it to the State Finals, Lower Merion would have to get by their old foes from Chester High School. All season long, Lower Merion had worn the number 27 on the back of their warm-ups. That was the number of points Chester had beaten Lower Merion by the year before.

The game was played at the Palestra in Philadelphia. Many of Philadelphia's best college basketball teams played at the Palestra. When

Kobe takes a foul shot against Chester High School.

Kobe Bryant holds the ball during an official timeout in the Pennsylvania State Title Game.

Lower Merion played Chester, thousands of fans packed into the old arena.

It was hot in the Palestra and the game was intense. After two action-packed halves, the game was tied and went into overtime. Kobe Bryant excelled in overtime. He scored eight points. The final two came on a breakaway. He drove straight down the lane and Chester defenders grabbed him and tugged at his jersey, trying to stop him, but they could not do it. He went up and dunked the ball to seal the win. The crowd exploded in applause.

Lower Merion went on to Hershey, Pennsylvania, to play Erie Cathedral Prep for the Pennsylvania State Championship. Erie Cathedral Prep was another well-coached, talented team. They stayed even with Lower Merion for most of the game. But at the end, Kobe Bryant grabbed a rebound late and fired a pass to teammate Omar Hatcher. Hatcher cruised in for the lay-up and the Aces went on to win the game. Lower Merion fans rushed the court. They celebrated that night and held a parade in Ardmore the next day.

The 1996 season had been a good one, so far. Kobe had led his team to the State Championship, and maintained a "B" average in school. As the

FACT

Kobe Bryant became the all-time leading scorer in Southeastern Pennsylvania high school history with 2,883 points. He broke the records held by NBA legend and Hall-of-Famer Wilt Chamberlain (2,359 points) and former St. Joseph's University star Carlin Warley (2,441 points).

Kobe cuts down the net after winning the Pennsylvania State Title.

weather turned warmer, Kobe Bryant was coming to terms with a very big decision.

He could have gone to almost any major college in the country. Duke, Kentucky, and Villanova were just a few of the schools that were actively recruiting him.

He could have gone to LaSalle University, where his father played and was now an assistant coach. But Bryant had much bigger plans.

On April 29, 1996, he called a news conference in the Lower Merion gym. He invited the entire student body. Reporters from television stations and newspapers all over the country showed up. At 2:35 p.m., Kobe Bryant stepped up to the microphone. Flashbulbs lit up the room while everyone waited for his decision. "I've decided to skip college and take my talent to the NBA," said Bryant.[5] Fellow students cheered wildly. But many experts questioned the decision.

"I think it's a total mistake," said Boston Celtics director of basketball development, Jon Jennings. "Kevin Garnett was the best high school player I ever saw, and I wouldn't have advised him to jump to the NBA. And Kobe is no Kevin Garnett."[6] Kevin Garnett was six foot ten inches tall. Most of the other players who had tried to go

FACT

The Pennsylvania State High School Championship game is played in Hershey, Pennsylvania. Milton S. Hershey founded Hershey, Pennsylvania, when he built a chocolate factory there in 1905. Before Milton Hershey came along, chocolate was a treat that only rich people could afford. He made the candy more available by pioneering the mass production of milk chocolate.

straight from high school to the NBA were big men.

Not long after he announced his intentions to play in the NBA, he signed a multi-million dollar deal to endorse an Adidas basketball sneaker. He also signed a contract to be represented by William Morris, a talent agency. That spring, he attended his senior prom with pop music and television star Brandy. Kobe Bryant was not just an ordinary high school basketball player any more.

Chapter 4
Joining the Lakers

Jerry West was one of the greatest players ever to play the guard position in the history of the National Basketball Association. He was named an All-American twice at West Virginia University. He also won an Olympic gold medal in Rome in 1960. He played for the Los Angeles Lakers throughout his professional career. He averaged 27 points per game and helped the Lakers win an NBA title in 1972. With his aggressive style and determination to win, he earned the nickname "Mr. Clutch."

Jerry West had basketball in his blood. The Lakers wanted to continue to use his talents when his playing career ended. He coached the team from 1976 to 1979. Then he was named general manager in 1982. He helped build the team that played in seven NBA finals during the 1980s.

A big part of Jerry West's job was deciding which young players would be great players in the NBA. In the days leading up to the 1996 NBA draft, West spent a lot of time watching college players work out. West had been around basketball a long time. He had played with many great players, including Wilt Chamberlain. He was not easily impressed. But he was impressed with Kobe Bryant.

West watched as Bryant jumped so high that he touched the top of the backboard square in a jumping drill. He held his own in one-on-one battles with Lakers great Michael Cooper and Mississippi State star Dontae Jones.

Kobe Bryant's agent later talked about West's reaction. "After the workout—I'll never forget it—when Jerry called up, he said it was the best workout he'd ever seen in his life. At the end of the conversation, he said, 'We've got to figure out a way to get him here.'"[1]

But getting Kobe Bryant to play for the Lakers would not be easy. Twenty-six teams would pick their new players before the Lakers even got a chance to select anyone on draft night. Bryant

Kobe celebrates winning the Pennsylvania State Title with teammate Jermaine Griffin (left) and Harry Middleton (center).

would almost certainly be gone by the time the Lakers had their turn.

On June 26, 1996, the NBA draft was held at the Meadowlands Arena in East Rutherford, New Jersey. A speedy guard from Georgetown University named Allen Iverson was drafted first by the Philadelphia 76ers. The college player of the year, Marcus Camby, was drafted second by the Toronto Raptors. Kobe Bryant sat with his family and waited.

Finally, NBA Commissioner David Stern announced Kobe Bryant as the thirteenth player selected in the draft. The team that chose him was the Charlotte Hornets. Bryant immediately put on a Hornets baseball cap. He walked up to the stage to shake hands with Commissioner Stern. He told a reporter how excited he was to be drafted and to be playing with Hornets star Larry Johnson.

But Jerry West still wanted to do whatever he could to get Bryant. The Hornets were willing to trade Bryant to the Lakers. But it was going to cost the Lakers. The Hornets wanted Vlade Divac.

Vlade Divac, a star from Yugoslavia, was the Lakers center, and he was a good player. If the Lakers traded Divac for Kobe, they would have to find someone just as good to take Divac's place.

FACT

Moses Malone was the first modern player to bypass college for professional basketball. In 1974, he was drafted by the American Basketball Association's Utah Stars. In his first year he averaged 18.8 points and 14.6 rebounds per game. His success led the Philadelphia 76ers and Atlanta Hawks to draft high school stars Darryl Dawkins and Bill Willoughby in 1975.

Kobe clowns around with high school teammate Jermaine Griffin.

The best center available was Shaquille O'Neal. O'Neal had been a college basketball star at Louisiana State University. He had gone on to lead the Orlando Magic to the NBA Finals in 1995. He was a free agent in 1996. Any team in the league could sign him. The Lakers got him, so Kobe Bryant would be starting his career as a Los Angeles Laker.

In addition to Bryant and O'Neal, the Lakers had enough talent to make them instant contenders in the Western Conference. They had star guards Eddie Jones and Nick Van Exel. Veterans Elden Campbell, Jerome Kersey, and Byron Scott were solid substitutes. If they could learn to play together as a team, they would be tough to beat.

The first half of Bryant's first year was hard. Sometimes he played well. But sometimes he looked like a struggling high school player. Nonetheless, Bryant was invited to participate in the NBA All-Star weekend in Cleveland, Ohio. He led all scorers with 31 points in the Rookie All-Star Game. The game's MVP Award went to Allen Iverson, as Iverson's East team beat Kobe Bryant's West team, 96–91. Then came the Slam-Dunk Contest, and Bryant soared.

Although he first started dunking with the

FACT

Shaquille O'Neal also spent some time overseas as a youngster. His father was a sergeant in the U.S. Army. He played his first season of organized basketball for a high school team on an army base in West Germany. It was there that he met his future college coach Dale Brown.

mini Dr. J rim when he was three, he was fourteen before he dunked a basketball through a regulation rim. His first dunk would not have won him any awards. "It was at my high school during one of the practices," he said. "Up till that point, I could barely touch the rim. Growing pains and things like that. The first one really wasn't a dunk. It was one of the things that you grab the rim and the ball happens to go in. After that, I was really excited, hyped up about it. Dunking was something I started working on."[2]

Some twenty thousand people chanted his name. Many celebrities, including his former prom date, Brandy, were there. Kobe Bryant got down to business with his very first dunk. It was a powerful dunk. But Bryant almost did not make it to the next round. He beat Denver's Darvin Ham by only one point.

Kobe Bryant found himself in the Finals with Chris Carr of the Minnesota Timberwolves and Michael Finley of the Dallas Mavericks. Carr put the pressure on with his first dunk. He started at halfcourt. Then he lofted the ball high into the air. He dashed forward, caught the ball on one bounce, did a 360-degree spin, and rammed the ball through the basket with both hands. The

Kobe Bryant speaks to an assembly of students at Lower Merion High School during a special ceremony retiring his old jersey number in February 2002.

judges, including Kobe Bryant's old hero, Dr. J, gave Carr 42 out of 50 possible total points.

Finley tried something out of the ordinary. He threw the ball high into the air, ran forward, and performed a half-cartwheel. He caught the ball and tried to throw down a monster dunk. The crowd held its breath but the ball clanged off the front of the rim and did not go in the hoop.

Then it was Bryant's turn again. He decided to repeat a dunk he had used to win a high school slam-dunk competition in Myrtle Beach, South Carolina, the year before.

He started from deep in the corner of the court. He took two dribbles, crouched down and pulled up the leg of his shorts. Then he took two quick dribbles, crossing from right to left. He took two long steps and he leaped into the air, clutching the ball in his left hand. He extended his right leg forward and his left leg back. He brought the ball down, and passed it through his legs, into his right hand. He swung his right arm like a windmill and slammed the ball through the hoop with his right hand. The ball shot downward toward the floor. Kobe Bryant landed and flexed his muscles.

The crowd exploded in applause. The judges

gave Bryant 49 out of 50 total points. It was the best score of the evening.

Kobe Bryant was crowned the 1997 Slam-Dunk Champion. He talked later about the importance of winning the contest. He also talked about meeting many of the all-time NBA greats who were honored that weekend in Cleveland. "It feels good to get out there and win the slam-dunk competition. That's something I've always dreamed about doing since I was a little kid. It's been a great experience since I got up here," he said. "I got a chance to see all the great players, talk to the young players, walking around, asking questions, getting advice on dunks. People are congratulating you on your first half of the season. It's been great, I've really enjoyed it. . . . Earl 'The Pearl' Monroe basically said 'keep your head up, keep working hard and good things will come. Good things come to those who wait.' Coming from him, that was something very special."[3]

Kobe Bryant spent most of the 1996–97 season learning how to play in the NBA. He was used to doing things himself in high school. Sitting on the bench was a new concept for him.

The Lakers came within one game of winning the Pacific Division title. Their first opponent in the playoffs were the Portland Trail Blazers. In the first two games of the series, Bryant played a total of only six minutes. But the Lakers won both games. In the third game, Bryant came off the bench to score 22 points. But the Lakers lost that game.

The Lakers eventually eliminated the Trail Blazers to move on and play the Utah Jazz.

The Jazz were led by John Stockton and Karl Malone. Stockton, one of the greatest point guards in NBA history, ran the Jazz offense and often found the open man with amazing no-look passes. Karl Malone definitely had to be one of the greatest power forwards in the history of the game. The two would often finish off fast breaks with Malone accepting a pass from Stockton and jamming a monstrous dunk.

In the first two games the Jazz overpowered the Lakers. They won both games on their home court to take a 2–0 lead in the series.

The Lakers won the next game in Los Angeles. But the Jazz came right back and won Game 4 with 42 points from Karl Malone. Game 5 would be back in Utah.

The Lakers fought hard. Shaquille O'Neal and Greg Ostertag, the Jazz center, pushed and leaned against each other underneath the basket.

Lakers forward Robert Horry shoved Jazz

Bryant slams home a monster dunk in the NBA's slam dunk competition in February 1997.

guard Jeff Hornacek. Horry was ejected from the game. Stockton and Malone ran the "pick and roll." The Lakers tried to answer at the other end of the court.

With only 11 seconds left in the game, the score was tied, 87–87. The Lakers had the ball and called a timeout. Lakers coach Del Harris designed a play that called for eighteen-year-old Kobe Bryant to take the last shot.

The ball was thrown in underneath the basket. Kobe Bryant dribbled upcourt. He was pressured hard by the Jazz defense, but he kept the ball under control. As the seconds ticked away, he pulled up just 14 feet from the basket. He launched a shot. The crowd watched and waited.

The shot fell short. In fact, it did not even hit the rim. Kobe Bryant's final shot was an airball. The game went into overtime.

Shaquille O'Neal had fouled out in the fourth quarter of regulation time. Kobe Bryant tried to lead his team as he had done so often in high school. But he shot three more airballs. The Jazz went on to win, 98–93.

Nick Van Exel later commented on the fact that Bryant was chosen to take the final shot. "Game 5 of the playoffs, we can't lose, that's a lot of pressure on Kobe. But, he's young, he thrives on the pressure situation."[4]

It was a disappointing way to end his first NBA season. The Lakers flew back to Los Angeles late that night. Those missed shots must have been on Bryant's mind the whole way. In fact, he would have the whole summer to think about them. But the mark of a true champion is how he or she responds to defeat.

Kobe Bryant responded well. Magic Johnson recalled being in a local gym the next morning when Bryant walked in to work out.

"That was just like me," Johnson said. "I loved seeing that from him. That's how I reacted, too. This is where he needs to be."[5]

Chapter 5

All-Star Player

As the 1997–98 NBA season opened, the Chicago Bulls were once again the favorites to win the NBA championship. They were going for their second "Threepeat" in the 1990s. They had Michael Jordan and Scottie Pippen on the court. Coach Phil Jackson directed from the bench. If the Lakers wanted to be the best team in the NBA, the Bulls were the team they would have to beat. If Kobe Bryant wanted to be the best player in the NBA, Michael Jordan was the player he would have to get past. On December 17, 1997, Bryant got his chance.

In front of more than twenty-four thousand fans in Chicago, Michael Jordan came out with something to prove. With his acrobatic moves to the hoop, he burned the Lakers for 13 points in the first quarter. He used some sharp shooting from the outside to score eight more points in the second quarter. The game was never close and the Bulls went on to win, 104–83. After the game, Jordan admitted that he was out to prove that Kobe was not yet ready to take his crown. "It was a challenge because of the hype," said Jordan. "But as a challenge, you try not to get carried away with the hype, not try to make it a one-on-one challenge with him. I thought a couple times it got that way, and I had to refrain."[1]

Kobe Bryant showed his respect for Michael Jordan by asking his advice on a particular move and Michael Jordan was happy to teach him. Bryant also performed well in the game. He scored 33 points while Jordan had 36.

"Whenever I have the chance to guard Michael Jordan, I want to guard him," Bryant said later. "I want him. The ultimate challenge."[2]

Kobe Bryant had worked hard during the off-season and it showed on the court. He was no longer a talented young player who came off the bench to help out. He was beginning to really contribute to the Lakers' success.

Bryant was one of the primary players in a

January showdown with the Orlando Magic. Forward Robert Horry was at the foul line shooting free throws. His second free throw clanged off the rim and did not go in. The Magic failed to cover the high-flying Bryant. Although he was actually drifting away from the ball, he reached back with his left hand and tipped the ball into the basket. He also made two foul shots in the final 10 seconds to give the Lakers the win.

A few nights later, the Lakers battled the Suns in Phoenix, Arizona. The Lakers were down by 16 points at one point in the game. But with pressure defense and good ball movement, they fought their way back. With 8:32 left in the game, they held a six-point lead over the Suns. Bryant took a pass on the right side of the court. He was about twenty-five feet from the basket, well beyond the three-point line. He squared up and launched a shot. Bang. It dropped through to put the Lakers up by nine. Bryant was beginning to show the confidence that he had played with in high school. Lakers coach Del Harris was impressed. "I don't want to take anything away from anyone," Harris said after the game. "It was a huge team effort. But Kobe was exceptional."[3]

Although Kobe Bryant was still the sixth man off the bench for the Lakers, his improved game

Kobe Bryant slips between two defenders in a game against the Cleveland Cavaliers in April 1998.

was winning fans all over the country. In February, those fans showed their appreciation, when they chose Bryant as a starter in the All-Star game. At only nineteen years old, Bryant would be the youngest All-Star in NBA history. "The interesting thing about him being selected for the All-Star game," Jerry West said, "we do not stuff ballots, period. These votes came from other people that obviously like to watch him play."[4]

The Lakers had done quite well in the first half of the season. They had a 34–11 record and they were only half a game behind the Seattle SuperSonics in the Pacific Division. Right before the All-Star Game, they avenged their earlier loss to the Bulls with a 112–87 win in Los Angeles.

Kobe Bryant was turning into a full-fledged star. *Sports Illustrated, Inside Sports,* and *Newsweek* were just a few of the national publications that ran feature stories on him. He had also appeared on the *Tonight Show with Jay Leno* and *Meet the Press.*

The 1998 All-Star Game was billed as another showdown between Kobe Bryant and Michael Jordan. Neither player disappointed. Although he was ill with the flu, Jordan of the East team scored 23 points and was named the game's MVP. Bryant led the West team with 18 points. The crowd at New York's Madison Square Garden watched the two superstars battle it out in the first half. Jordan blew by Bryant early on with a head fake and scored on a finger roll. Bryant came right back and hit two three-point shots.

Kobe Bryant added a play that reminded some of Magic Johnson when he came down the right side of the court on a fast break. He whipped the ball behind his back as though he was going to pass to a teammate. But he did not pass it. He continued dribbling with the same hand. The move froze the defense, and Bryant launched a hook shot that hit nothing but net.

Michael Jordan enjoyed his showdown with Kobe Bryant. "It was a good battle. It was fun. He attacked," Jordan said. "The hype was me vs. him. I knew I wasn't 100 percent and he was, and he was biting at the bit. I was just glad that I was able to fight him off."[5]

During the second half of the 1997–98 season Bryant did not play as well as he had been playing. Teams guarded him more closely. And playing more minutes was beginning to wear him down. He played through the difficulties, though,

FACT

With just five seconds to go in Game 6, Michael Jordan hit a jump shot that gave the Chicago Bulls an 87–86 victory over the Utah Jazz. The win gave the Bulls their sixth NBA Title of the 90s. Jordan was also named the MVP of the NBA Finals for the sixth time. His 5,987 playoff points broke the record that was previously held by Kareem Abdul-Jabbar.

and on March 23, he scored 23 points in a 107–86 defeat of the Denver Nuggets. "I just slowed my moves up a little bit," Kobe said after the game. "Tonight, I tried to use my body more, use my size, whether I was backing in or posting up or whatever. I think teams had gotten so used to me facing the basket."[6]

The Lakers really hit their stride late in the year. They won 22 of their last 25 games. They then took on the Portland Trail Blazers in the first round of the playoffs.

The Lakers played well. Kobe Bryant was the star in the fourth quarter of Game 2. He drove past Portland stars Isaiah Rider and Rasheed Wallace to score 11 points in a 104–102 victory. "Me and Rasheed have been going at each other since high school," Bryant said afterward. "We're pretty used to that matchup."[7]

The Lakers finished off the Trail Blazers and went on to sweep the Seattle SuperSonics in four games. Bryant sat out two of those games with the flu.

The Lakers then moved on to take on the Utah Jazz. Bryant was determined to make people forget about the previous year's airballs. But it was not to be.

Utah's veteran players made the Lakers look

young and inexperienced. They swept the Lakers in four games. Shaquille O'Neal expressed his frustrations afterward. "Guys just have to step up," he said "They have to find out what's most important to them. If they don't want to play, then they need to ask for a trade. If they don't want to play, then get off my team."[8]

Chapter 6
Welcome Dennis Rodman

Ever since he was a little boy, Kobe Bryant has been able to focus on one thing. He has spent hour after hour working hard to become the best basketball player he can be. Unlike high school, however, the NBA is a business. And the business side of the NBA disrupted Kobe's focus on the game in 1998.

The players and owners disagreed about their contracts and much of the first half of the 1998–1999 season was cancelled.

The disagreement was settled in early January and the NBA season was ready to start. But it would start without the league's greatest player. Michael Jordan called a press conference in Chicago to announce his retirement.

His teammate Scottie Pippen was traded to the Houston Rockets. Their flashy rebounding leader, Dennis Rodman, was released from the team. The Chicago Bulls were officially broken up. For the first time in years, the NBA title was up for grabs.

Kobe Bryant was optimistic about his team's chances in the upcoming shortened season. But he also knew the Lakers had a lot of work ahead of them. "We've got some talented basketball players," he said. "But we all know talent's not going to win you a championship anyway. Whether you have ten talented players or five talented players, you're going to have to get the work done on the basketball court."[1]

The Lakers did have a solid lineup coming into the season. They had traded Nick Van Exel in the offseason. But Kobe and Eddie Jones still gave them a good one-two punch at guard. Rick Fox, Corie Blount, and Elden Campbell all played the forward position. And, of course, they had Shaquille O'Neal. What they lacked was a strong power forward—someone who could help Shaq grab rebounds and play solid defense.

Early in the season, they did not play well. In late February, they lost three games in a row and had a 6–6 record. The Lakers knew they needed help. There was one player out there who could help them, but it would be a gamble to sign him. His name was Dennis Rodman.

The first NBA team Rodman had played for was the Detroit Pistons. Rodman won two NBA titles with the Pistons. He then went on to play for the San Antonio Spurs. He started to dye his hair different colors and say outrageous things in interviews. Then he played for the Bulls and his rebounding and defensive skills helped them win championships. But his behavior on and off the court was sometimes a distraction.

"It's going to take some getting used to," Bryant said about Rodman. "I've never experienced anything exactly like this. He's not a role model off the court, but he's a great player and you can learn a lot by just observing him [on the court]."[2]

Rodman chose to wear number 73 for the Lakers. Seven represented the number of rebounding titles he had won. Three represented the number of consecutive NBA titles he had won with the Chicago Bulls.

One day after signing Rodman, the Lakers made another big change. Head coach Del Harris was replaced by Kurt Rambis.

Rodman contributed right away. He had 11 rebounds and 6 assists as the Lakers beat the

Clippers. Then he had 10 rebounds and played smothering defense against Charles Barkley in a win over the Houston Rockets.

The Los Angeles fans loved Rodman's wacky personality, and he was not shy about his abilities. "This team needs me," he said. "I'm bringing excitement, a lot of hustle and leadership. I never thought I'd say that."³

In early March the Lakers made one more big change in an effort to improve their chance of winning the title. They traded all-star guard Eddie Jones and forward Elden Campbell to the Charlotte Hornets for Glen Rice. Rice was one of the best shooting guards in the league. The move gave the Lakers three strong offensive weapons. But first they would have to learn to play together.

On the night of March 21, the Academy Awards were held in Los Angeles. Earlier that day, Kobe Bryant had put on a show of his own. The Lakers faced the Orlando Magic and were soundly beaten in the first half. They trailed 63–43 at halftime.

But Kobe Bryant fueled a comeback. His sharp shooting burned up the nets. He scored 33 points after halftime and finished with 38 points in the game. The Lakers went on to beat the Magic, 115–104.

FACT

Kurt Rambis started out his professional career playing in Greece. He went on to play seven seasons for the Los Angeles Lakers. He won NBA titles with the team in 1982, 1985, 1987, and 1988. With his thick, dark-rimmed glasses and floppy hair, he earned the nickname "Clark Kent."

A month after their trade for Rice, the Lakers found themselves with a 22–12 record. They were in second place in their division. Although the addition of Dennis Rodman was helping the Lakers win games, his bad behavior on and off the court was becoming a distraction. As many people had feared, he received many technical fouls and he missed games without giving reasons. Many of his teammates were becoming frustrated with Rodman. "We get called a party team all the time, and that's not what all of us do," Bryant said. "Some of us take this seriously."[4]

Despite his contributions on the court, the Lakers had no choice but to let Dennis Rodman go.

They opened the playoffs with a best-of-five series against the Houston Rockets. In addition to Scottie Pippen and Charles Barkley, the Rockets featured veteran stars Clyde Drexler and Hakeem Olajuwon. Barkley was hungry for the title that had so far eluded him. Pippen was eager to prove that he could win a title on a team without Michael Jordan.

The Rockets were poised to take Game 1 of the series. They came back from a fourth quarter deficit to take a one-point lead in the game. They had the ball with less than 30 seconds left. Scottie Pippen tried to dribble some time off the clock, but he lost control of the ball. The Lakers' Derek Fisher pounced on it and called timeout with 7.6 seconds left.

During the timeout, Rambis called a play for Kobe Bryant. Bryant caught the ball as time ticked away. He drove to the basket but lost his balance. The ball came loose. As the rest of the players scrambled for the ball, the whistle blew. Bryant had been fouled.

Lakers fans held their breath as Bryant stepped to the foul line. He made the first shot to tie the game. He dribbled calmly and made the second one as well. That put the Lakers up by one point. The Rockets tried to win the game with a last second shot. But Shaquille O'Neal blocked Cuttino Mobley's shot.

The Rockets put up little resistance for the remainder of the series. The Lakers cruised into the second round of the playoffs. "I've been saying it for a while now—this team is coming together," said Kurt Rambis. "We're a team that had a huge upside potential coming into the playoffs. And we still haven't played our best game yet."[5]

To advance to the Finals, the Lakers would have to get by the San Antonio Spurs. The Spurs were led by David Robinson and rookie sensation

Tim Duncan. In the first game of the series, they used defense to set the tone.

Robinson and Duncan got the best of Shaquille O'Neal. Will Perdue and Malik Rose pitched in to give the Lakers a tough time. Although Bryant, Rice, and O'Neal each scored 21 points, the Spurs took Game 1.

In Game 2, the Lakers came out swinging. They took an early 24–10 lead, but the Spurs battled back. Down the stretch, Bryant tried to take over. "He was operating on pick-and-rolls and it was tough for us to deal with him," said Elliot later.[6]

Late in the game, the Spurs led by two points. With Elliot covering him tightly, Kobe drove hard down the lane and hit a running shot. That tied the score at 71.

The Spurs went back up, 75–73, but the Lakers had the ball. With only 36 seconds left, Kobe Bryant launched a long three-point shot.

He nailed it and the Lakers were up by one point. Then, with only 18 seconds left, Bryant was fouled. He had a chance to increase the Lakers' lead. But both shots bounced off the rim. The Spurs went right to Tim Duncan, and he nailed a short jump-hook.

Bryant tried to inbound the ball quickly for the

Kobe Bryant dribbles around Byron Russell of the Utah Jazz.

Lakers. The pass bounced off a teammate's head. The Spurs hit two more free throws to put them up by three. Bryant launched a thirty-foot shot at the buzzer to try to tie the game, but it fell short. The Spurs walked away with a 79–76 win.

Shaquille O'Neal summed up the game this way: "We have to play smart. There [is] no secret. We beat ourselves. We had it, and we fell again. We made too many mistakes down the stretch."[7]

Although they traveled back to Los Angeles to continue the series, the Lakers could not stop the Spurs. They lost both games and, for the second straight year, the Lakers were swept out of the playoffs in four games.

Magic Johnson had watched the final game from a courtside seat. "I'm embarrassed," he said. "And they should be embarrassed. This is the second year in a row we've gotten swept in the playoffs. When are we going to learn?"[8]

The Lakers were going to need help learning. Not long after they were swept from the playoffs, they made a move to bring in a great teacher and a proven winner: They hired Michael Jordan's old coach, Phil Jackson.

Chapter 7

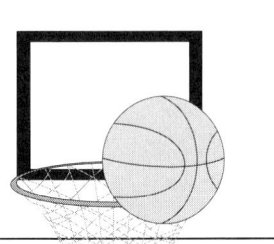

The Champs!

Before becoming the coach of the Chicago Bulls, Phil Jackson had played for many years in the NBA. After starring at the University of North Dakota, he played thirteen seasons with the New York Knicks and New Jersey Nets. He sat out the Knicks' 1969–70 championship season with a back injury. But the Knicks used him as an assistant coach that year. That was when he discovered a love for coaching.

After coaching in the Continental Basketball Association (CBA), he returned to the NBA as an assistant for the Chicago Bulls. He was named the Bulls' head coach in 1989.

Jackson soon earned the nickname the

"Zenmaster." He introduced his interest in meditation and Eastern religions to his players. He coached a system called the triangle offense. The triangle was an offense that took advantage of the explosive one-on-one skills of Michael Jordan. Jackson planned on taking advantage of Kobe Bryant's one-on-one skills in the same way in Los Angeles.

Steve Kerr, a former Bulls player, commented on how Jackson got the most out of all his players in Chicago. "He always had a knack for making everybody on the team feel like he was an important cog, whether it was Michael Jordan or anybody else down the line. That was his strength as a coach—getting the most out of every single player and making them play as a team."[1]

Scottie Pippen, the Bulls' other star on their six title teams, also thought the addition of Coach Jackson would help Kobe Bryant. He said, "Phil [Coach Jackson] is going to teach him how to let the game come to him instead of always forcing the issue."[2]

Preseason expectations were high again in Los Angeles. But Kobe Bryant would have to learn to be patient. For the second time in his career, a preseason injury kept him out of action until early December.

FACT

The word Zen means "meditation" in Japanese. Zen Buddhism is usually associated with the religious history of China and Japan. Some people believe that Zen Buddhism was actually started in India and was brought to China by a monk named Bodhidharma in 520 A.D.

Although he played for only thirty minutes in his first game back, he scored 19 points in a victory over the Golden State Warriors. He got into the flow early. On one possession, he dribbled behind his back and blew by a Warriors defender. He launched a shot that sailed over the arm of the Warriors' center and banked in.

Bryant's injury was to his shooting hand. While he waited for it to heal, he practiced with his left hand. "I'm going to use it a lot," he promised. "It's another weapon I have down on the block, posting up."[3]

The Lakers cruised through the first part of the season. By Christmas, they had a 22–5 record.

Bryant's skills began to flourish under the triangle offense. In a game against Atlanta, he matched shots with the Hawks' Isaiah Rider. He scored 30 and Rider scored 33. "We went back and forth at each other, both of us saying nice play, things like that. Kobe and me don't talk trash," Rider said afterward. "I scored more points; he played a better game."[4]

In a game against the Minnesota Timberwolves, Bryant showed some of the same body control that made Michael Jordan so great. He drove to the basket hard and jumped high to dunk the ball. The Timberwolves' seven-foot center came over to block the shot. Kobe brought the ball down and waited for the defender to bang into him. When he did, Bryant put the ball in the basket. He also went to the line for a foul shot. Coach Jackson liked what he was seeing. But he also knew that Kobe had room to improve.

"He's had some really good moments, but sometimes he gets enamored with trying to score too often," he said. "I still feel the need for some self-sacrifice out there on the court, some moments when he's got to be a guard in the guard sense of organizing the team and getting the offense to run the right way."[5]

In a win against the Celtics, Kobe scored 27 points and added 4 rebounds, 4 assists, and 4 steals.

On one play, he drove down the lane and the Celtics' defense closed in to trap him. Bryant whipped a pass behind his back to Shaquille O'Neal and O'Neal went up for the easy slam-dunk.

On another play, he drove in from the wing and dribbled behind his back. Celtics guard Kenny Anderson met him. Bryant then dribbled between his legs and moved into the lane. He tossed up a one-handed shot over two Celtics defenders for the bucket.

People know Michael Jordan as a player who made acrobatic moves and spectacular slam-dunks. But many people do not know that the Bulls star also worked hard to become one of the greatest defensive players in the league. Kobe Bryant was also focused on defense. In February, he had the opportunity to demonstrate his defensive abilities. The Lakers were in Philadelphia to take on the 76ers. The Sixers were led by one of the most explosive scorers in the game, guard Allen Iverson.

To stop Iverson, Bryant used his height advantage. He forced the Sixers' guard to take bad shots and held him scoreless in the second half. In the fourth quarter, he blocked three of Iverson's shots. Bryant also scored the final six points of the game after O'Neal fouled out. The Lakers went on to win, 87–84.

"That's the difference in our club," Bryant said afterward. "We always had the offensive firepower, but defense is how you win."[6]

With the help of an MVP-season from Shaquille O'Neal, the Lakers finished the regular season with a 67–15 record. They took on the young and talented Sacramento Kings in the first round of the playoffs.

O'Neal scored 46 points and pulled down 17

rebounds in a 117–107 win in Game 1. In Game 2, the Kings tried harder to slow down O'Neal. But then they ran into Kobe Bryant.

Bryant nailed some very long three-point shots. One was launched from 34 feet away with Kings guard Nick Anderson right in his face. He also switched roles with O'Neal at one point. Shaq lobbed an alley-oop pass and Bryant slammed it through the basket. Bryant finished with 32 points in the 113–89 blowout of the Kings. "We spent a lot of time talking about Shaq," Kings coach Rick Adelman said later. "We should have spent more time talking about Kobe. They took it to us."[7]

Phil Jackson noticed that the more teams paid attention to O'Neal, the more opportunities Kobe Bryant had to score. "They were in Shaq's lap," he said. "They were determined not to let him get the ball, and that left some of our other guys open, including Kobe."[8]

The Lakers eventually beat the Kings in five games. The Lakers eliminated the Phoenix Suns in the next series. That brought on a showdown with the Portland Trail Blazers in the Western Conference Finals.

The Blazers had finished the regular season with the second best record in the league. Many people had predicted this matchup in the finals

Kobe Bryant takes a jump shot against the Sacramento Kings.

before the season started. Arvydas Sabonis, Rasheed Wallace, and Brian Grant were three big players that could challenge Shaquille O'Neal and the Lakers' forwards. They also had Scottie Pippen and Steve Smith running the offense.

The Lakers took Game 1. In Game 2, Rasheed Wallace poured in 29 points to lead the Blazers to a 106–77 blowout. The series was getting emotional. Scottie Pippen questioned whether the young Lakers had what it took to get to the Finals. "I think we all know Shaq and Kobe are players who have been around the game. But from a playoff standpoint, they're still a little bit young," Pippen said. "They don't know what it is to be in that position. They don't really know how to get themselves out of that position. That's an opportunity for us to take advantage of them and push them in a corner and see how they react."[9]

O'Neal and Bryant reacted well. But they got much-needed help from playoff veteran Ron Harper. In the closing minutes of Game 3 he stole the ball from Pippen. He cruised in to score the go-ahead basket in a 93–91 win. In Game 4 he had 18 points and 7 rebounds in a 103–91 win.

Although they trailed in the series three games to one, Portland would not go away easily. They beat the Lakers twice in a row to send the series to a seventh game in Los Angeles.

The Blazers' big men started Game 7 swarming all over Shaquille O'Neal. They double-teamed him and sometimes triple-teamed him when he touched the ball. The Lakers' outside shots clanged off the rim. They found themselves trailing, 23–16, at the end of the first quarter.

In the second half, Portland turned up the heat. They outscored the Lakers 18–2 in one stretch, and built a 68–53 lead. Phil Jackson knew his team was in trouble. He called a timeout and tried to wake his players up. "Portland stuck us for nine straight possessions," he said later. "I called timeout and jumped in their faces and they responded."[10] He also told the Lakers to "forget Shaq."[11] The Blazers' big men were guarding him too tightly. If they were going to come back, they needed someone else to step up. Brian Shaw, Robert Horry, and Kobe Bryant all stepped up. They started to hit the big baskets and they chipped away at the Portland lead. On their end, the Blazers went cold.

Shaquille O'Neal scored 9 of his 18 points in the fourth quarter to help the Lakers take the lead. With only a four-point lead and less than a minute left, Kobe Bryant found himself with a breakaway opportunity. The middle of the lane was wide open. He dribbled toward it but then saw O'Neal open underneath. He lobbed an alley-oop pass. At first, Bryant thought he threw it too high. It looked like it was going over the backboard. Then he relaxed and a big smile came across his face. The Los Angeles crowd erupted in applause as O'Neal leaped into the air with his mighty arm extended. He caught the pass and rammed the ball through the rim. The Lakers were on their way to the NBA Finals.

"It was a chance for an easy bucket," said O'Neal. "And I didn't get any easy buckets all night."[12]

Kobe Bryant and Shaquille O'Neal were one step closer to their first NBA title ring. But first, they would have to get by the Indiana Pacers. Reggie Miller was the star of the Pacers. He was quick and smart. He could get open without the ball and nail down long three-point shots. Pacers' coach Larry Bird knew something about the NBA Finals. As a player for the Boston Celtics, he battled Magic Johnson and the Lakers. Kobe Bryant was enthusiastic about playing for an NBA title. "I've waited all of my life to get to the Finals," the twenty-one-year-old said. "It's a dream come true. To have it happen so fast, I've been very fortunate.

FACT

In the early 1970s, the American Basketball Association (ABA) was a rival league to the NBA. When the 1976–77 season started, the ABA went out of existence. Four teams from the ABA joined the NBA. They were the San Antonio Spurs, Denver Nuggets, Indiana Pacers, and New York Nets. (Later the Nets were renamed the New Jersey Nets and moved from Long Island, New York, to East Rutherford, New Jersey). In 1999, the San Antonio Spurs became the first ABA team to win an NBA title.

Some players have been in this league a long time and haven't gotten to this point."[13]

The Lakers won Game 1 easily and they finished off the Pacers in Game 2 after Kobe Bryant sprained his ankle. But Game 3 proved that the Lakers needed Kobe Bryant healthy as the Pacers beat the Lakers, 100–91.

Bryant's ankle was still sore before Game 4. But he answered all questions when he dominated the overtime period of that game. The 120–118 victory gave his team a commanding 3 games to 1 lead in the series. The Lakers were on their way. "It was just realizing the time to attack," he said after scoring eight of his twenty-eight points in overtime. "Phil brought it to me in a different light. It was more kind of relaxing, going with the flow of the game, just investigating the floor really. You penetrate. You know that you can get to that spot, so you say, 'OK, I know I can get there, I'll come back there later, I might come back there in the fourth quarter.' Little mind games that you play. That's how he approached it with me. It was just so interesting. He taught me very, very well. That's all I'm doing, is just attacking at the right time."[14]

In the final game of the series, the Lakers came from behind to beat the Pacers, 116–111.

Bryant had 26 points and 10 rebounds. Shaquille O'Neal had 41 points and 12 rebounds.

Shaquille O'Neal won the Most Valuable Player Award for the Finals. He had also been named the NBA's regular season MVP and the All-Star Game MVP. Kobe Bryant was just pleased to have a championship ring. Although he was only twenty-one years old, it seemed like he had waited and worked a long time for it. "I was upset that we kept losing in the playoffs. I was upset with people talking about my game as far as not being a team player or being great defensively. I just wanted to make a change. I wanted to prove, you know, that what they were saying was wrong."[15]

Whatever they said about Kobe Bryant, it was a fact that at the end of the 2000 NBA season he had an NBA championship ring. He had also been named to the NBA All-Defensive Team, had played on the NBA All-Star Team twice, and had won the Slam-Dunk Championship.

Chapter 8

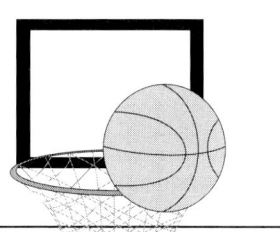

Kobe off the Court

While his success on the court would overwhelm some, Kobe Bryant has been able to stay focused on the important things in life. Family is important to him. When he first moved to Los Angeles, his mother and father moved in with him. They kept him updated on his sisters' volleyball games back in Philadelphia.

Bryant keeps busy with many business and charity organizations off the court. "I like getting out there for promotional appearances and having a good time and meeting people," he says. "I like to see the end product, and I take pride in it. I want my product to be one of the best things out there. And I love going in front of the cameras

Kobe Bryant enjoys some time away from the court with his old high school coach, Gregg Downer.

and learning something new. But I understand basketball is what got me here and on top of that, I love to do it so much that it will always be my focal point."[1]

With his busy schedule, Kobe Bryant does not get much time to relax. When he does, he likes to watch television shows like *Living Single* and *Jamie Foxx*. He also likes to read. He started Kobe's Reading Club on his Web site. He encourages kids to e-mail him book reports on some of their favorite books.

He really likes rap music, and he even recorded his own album called "Visions" in 2000. He performed his single K.O.B.E. with super-model Tyra Banks on the NBA TeamUp Celebration television special. TeamUp recognizes the volunteer efforts of thousands of teens.

But Kobe Bryant does not really like to go out late when he's on the road. "I've never really been a club person," he says. "I really like to spend time with my family and friends, outside of the lights and all that."[2]

Of course, if he keeps adding to his personal awards and team championships, staying outside of the spotlight is going to be very difficult for Kobe Bryant.

Chapter 9

The 2000-2001 Season

As the 2000–2001 NBA season opened, the Los Angeles Lakers were firmly established as the team to beat. Nonetheless, the team had still made moves in the offseason to improve. They traded for power forward Horace Grant, another former Bulls star. They also signed Isaiah "J.R." Rider as a free agent. Other teams in the league made moves in the offseason to try to challenge the Lakers.

"All teams are looking to get as big as they can," Portland coach Mike Dunleavy said. "The Lakers are the champions, so you target your needs for them."[1]

The Lakers were equally determined to repeat. Shaquille O'Neal summed up his approach to the new season. "Winning championship trophies is like having one car," he said. "It's not enough for me."[2]

Kobe Bryant worked hard in the offseason. The Lakers traded sharpshooter Glen Rice to the New York Knicks, and Bryant would have to make up for the loss of Rice. He took some two thousand outside shots a day over the summer. "I worked extremely hard this summer," he said. "It seems now like I can get my shot any time."[3]

Phil Jackson knew that despite all of Kobe Bryant's early accomplishments, he was eager to take his game to an even higher level. And Jackson was concerned that Bryant sometimes tried to do too much on his own. "Kobe is occasionally going to go off on one of his tears a little too much," Jackson said. "But he will do that. He's going to test the waters to see how it is out there. But he finds his way back."[4]

In a December matchup against the Golden State Warriors, Bryant scored 51 points. But the Warriors' Antawn Jamison also scored 51. The Lakers lost in overtime.

The first half of the 2000–2001 season saw Shaquille O'Neal battling injuries. Kobe Bryant was forced to step up his scoring. In fact, he led the NBA in scoring halfway through the season

FACT

Kobe's fan club is called the Kobe Klub. Members pay dues, but the money is donated to the Kobe Bryant Foundation. This is a group that donates all of the money it raises to at-risk young people in the Los Angeles area.

Kobe Bryant goes up for a dunk in a game against the Minnesota Timberwolves.

and was again one of the leading vote-getters for the NBA All-Star Game.

The Lakers were in the spotlight much of the year. Although their record was one of the best in the league, rumors were spreading that Kobe Bryant and Shaquille O'Neal were not getting along well.

Bryant sprained his ankle on March 21 and missed nine games. He came back in impressive style. He shut down Jason Kidd and the Phoenix Suns in a 106–80 win. He also tied his career high with 6 steals.

"They are getting ready," said Phil Jackson afterward. "We talked about playoff intensity today, and they played with that intensity. It was a breakout game for us."[5]

That intensity continued into the playoffs, as the Lakers swept the Portland Trail Blazers (3–0), Sacramento Kings (4–0), and San Antonio Spurs (4–0) to win the Western Conference title.

In the Finals, Kobe Bryant and the Lakers met Allen Iverson and the Philadelphia 76ers. The Sixers put up a good fight. They won one game, but Los Angeles proved to be too much for them. The Lakers became NBA Champions for the second year in a row, winning the Finals four games to one.

Chapter Notes

Chapter 1. A Star Is Born

1. Greg Boeck, "O'Neal Rallies Lakers 89-84, Los Angeles Heads to Finals Thanks to Torrid 4th Quarter," *USA Today*, June 5, 2000, p. 1C.

2. Tim Kawakami, "Bryant Says Nothing Will Keep Him from Game 4," *Los Angeles Times*, June 14, 2000, p. C-1.

3. Ibid.

4. Associated Press, "Kobe Just Super as Lakers Win in OT," *The Sporting News*, June 14, 2000, http://www.sportingnews.com (May 1, 2001).

5. Ibid.

6. Bill Plaschke, "That Was No Dream, That Was Kobe," *Los Angeles Times*, June 15, 2000, p. C-1.

7. Associated Press, "Kobe Just Super as Lakers Win in OT."

8. Greg Boeck, "Kobe Rises Into His Own Status as Elite Superstar," *USA Today*, June 16, 2000, p. 1C.

9. Ibid.

Chapter 2. Childhood

1. Helene Elliott, "Kobe Bryant Humbly Begins His Jump from Preps to Pros," *Los Angeles Times*, October 15, 1996, p. C-1.

2. Ian Thomsen, "Show Time! Is Kobe Bryant the Second Coming of Magic or Michael?," *Sports Illustrated*, April 27, 1998, p. 40.

3. Ibid.

4. Ibid.

5. Elliott. p. C-1.

6. Ibid.

Chapter 3. State Champ

1. Helene Elliott, "Kobe Bryant Humbly Begins His Jump from Preps to Pros," *Los Angeles Times*, October 15, 1996, p. C-1.

2. Author's interview with Michael Egan, December 16, 2000.

3. Ibid.

4. Ibid.

5. Michael Bamberger, "School's Out, Philadelphia Schoolboy Bryant Is Headed Straight for the NBA," *Sports Illustrated*, May 6, 1996, p. 50.

6. Ibid.

Chapter 4. Joining the Lakers

1. Mark Heisler, "The Kid's Got It!," *Los Angeles Times*, February 6, 1998, p. C-1.

2. "1997 NBA All-Star Weekend," February 8, 1997, <http://www.asapsports.com> (December 18, 2000).

3. Mark Heisler, "King Kobe; At 18 Lakers' Bryant Steals the Show by Becoming Youngest to Win Slam-Dunk Contest and Scoring 31 Points in Rookie All-Star Game," *Los Angeles Times*, February 6, 1997, p. C-6.

4. Tim Kawakami, "Lakers Get Aired Out," *Los Angeles Times*, May 13, 1997, p. C-1.

5. Ian Thomsen, "Show Time! Is Kobe Bryant the Second Coming of Magic or Michael?," *Sports Illustrated*, April 27, 1998, p. 40.

Chapter 5. All-Star Player

1. Scott Howard-Cooper, "Lakers Are Victims of Jordan Takeover," *Los Angeles Times*, December 18, 1997, p. C-1.

2. Ibid.

3. Scott Howard-Cooper, "Bryant Is a Big Shot for Lakers," *Los Angeles Times*, January 22, 1998, p. C-1.

4. Mark Heisler, "The Kid's Got It," *Los Angeles Times*, February 6, 1998, p. C-1.

5. Associated Press, "No Heir to Air," *Los Angeles Times*, February 9, 1998, p. C-1.

6. Scott Howard-Cooper, "Bryant Finds Touch Again," *Los Angeles Times*, March 24, 1998, p. C-1.

7. David Leon Moore, "Bryant Getting a Feel for Postseason, Many Lessons Remain to Be Learned," *USA Today*, April 28, 1998, p. 9C.

8. Greg Boeck, "Embarrassed Lakers to Look Within for Answers," *USA Today*, May 26, 1998, p. 14C.

Chapter 6. Welcome Dennis Rodman

1. J. A. Adande, "Good Sign for Lakers?," *Los Angeles Times*, January 20, 1999, p. D-1.

2. David DuPree, "Showtime's Plot Thickens," *USA Today*, March 1, 1999, p. 1C.

3. Ibid.

4. "Rodman Says He's Key to Lakers' Title Hopes," *USA Today*, April 5, 1999, p. 9C.

5. David Leon Moore, "Lakers Rip Rockets 110–98 to go up 2–0," *USA Today*, May 12, 1999, p. 10C.

6. David DuPree, "Bryant Wins Battle but Loses the War in Lakers' Defeat," *USA Today*, May 21, 1999, p. 14C.

7. Ibid.

8. Greg Boeck, "Swept Again, Lakers' Search for Answers Continues," *USA Today*, May 24, 1999, p. 10C.

Chapter 7. The Champs!

1. David DuPree, "Lakers Can Expect Big Changes, Jackson Brings Philosophy That Will Mold a True Team," *USA Today*, June 17, 1999, p. 3C.

2. David DuPree, "In Key Win, Bryant Shows He's at Top of His Game," *USA Today*, March 2, 2000, p. 1C.

3. Greg Boeck, "Will Triangle Offense Create Enough Shots to Appease L.A. Duo?," *USA Today*, December 3, 1999, p. 1C.

4. David DuPree, "Jackson's Team a Hit on the Road, Bryant and O'Neal Announce L.A.'s Arrival During Their Perfect Tour," *USA Today*, December 23, 1999, p. 3C.

5. Ibid.

6. Greg Boeck, "Bryant Outplays Iverson in Battle of Philly All-Stars," *USA Today*, February 21, 2000, p. 4C.

7. Greg Boeck, "O'Neal, Bryant Guard Against Letdown as Lakers Roll 113–89," *USA Today*, April 28, 2000, p. 15C.

8. Ibid.

9. Greg Boeck, "Blazers, Lakers Play Mental Games too, Portland 'Jackals' Shrug off Jackson," *USA Today*, May 26, 2000, p. 13C.

10. Greg Boeck, "O'Neal Gets the Right Stuff from Bryant," *USA Today*, June 5, 2000, p. 1C.

11. Ibid.

12. Ibid.

13. Kevin Jackson, "Finals Preview," June 2000, <http://www.espn.com> (December 18, 2000).

14. David DuPree, "Lakers Return to Top of NBA Finals, MVP O'Neal Scores 41 in 116–111 Win vs. Pacers," *USA Today*, June 20, 2000, p. 1C.

15. Greg Boeck, "Kobe Rises into His Own Status as Elite Superstar," *USA Today*, June 16, 2000, p. 1C.

Chapter 8. Kobe off the Court

1. Helene Elliott, "Ahead of the Class; Kobe Bryant Humbly Begins His Jump from Preps to Pros," *Los Angeles Times*, October 15, 1996, p. C-1.

2. Scott Howard-Cooper, "Reaching for the Sky," *Los Angeles Times*, March 10, 1997, p. E-1.

Chapter 9. The 2000–2001 Season

1. David DuPree, "Encore for Lakers? L.A. Has Retooled for a Chance at Another NBA Title," *USA Today*, October 31, 2000, p. 1C.

2. Ibid.

3. Ibid.

4. Ibid.

5. John Nadel, "Lakers Feeling Good as Playoffs Approach," *Intelligencer Journal*, April 12, 2001, p. 1C.

Career Statistics

YEAR	TEAM	GP	FG%	Reb.	Ast.	Stl.	Blk.	Pts.	Avg.
1996–97	Lakers	71	.417	132	91	49	23	539	7.6
1997–98	Lakers	79	.428	242	199	74	40	1,220	15.4
1998–99	Lakers	50	.465	264	190	72	50	996	19.9
1999–00	Lakers	66	.468	416	323	106	62	1,485	22.5
2000–01	Lakers	68	.409	399	338	114	43	1,938	28.5
2001–02	Lakers	80	.469	441	438	118	35	2,019	25.2
Totals		414	.458	1,894	1,579	533	253	8,197	19.8

GP—Games Played
FG%—Field Goal Percentage
Reb.—Rebounds
Ast.—Assists
Stl.—Steals
Blk.—Blocks
Pts.—Points Scored
Avg.—Points per Game

Where to Write Kobe Bryant

Mr. Kobe Bryant
c/o Los Angeles Lakers
Great Western Forum
3900 W. Manchester Blvd.
Inglewood CA, 90305

On the Internet at:

The NBA's Official Web Site
<http://www.nba.com/playerfile/kobe_bryant.html>

The Los Angeles Lakers' Official Web Site
<http://www.nba.com/lakers>

Index

A
Adelman, Rick, 79
Adidas, 42
All-Star Game (1997), 48–52
All-Star Game (1998), 61–62
American Basketball Association (ABA), 83
Ardmore, Pennsylvania, 8, 25

B
Bala Cynwyd Middle School, 29
Barkley, Charles, 68, 69
Bird, Larry, 15, 83
Boston Celtics, 77
Bryant, Joe (father), 19–21, 23, 26
Bryant, Kobe
    1997-98 NBA season, 57–64
    1998-99 NBA season, 65–73
    1999-00 NBA season, 9, 75–85
    2000-01 NBA season, 9–17, 90–92
    All-Star challenge, 57–62
    all-time leading scorer, 39
    career statistics, 99
    childhood of, 20–28
    first NBA season, 52–56
    high school to NBA, 41–42
    joining the Lakers, 44–48
    NBA title ring, 83–85
    NBA's Slam-Dunk Champion, 48–52
    off the court, 86–88
    season injuries, 10–12, 75–76, 92
    state high school championship, 30–40
    winning the NBA championship, 9–17, 90–92
    youngest All-Star, 8, 17–18, 61
Bryant, Pam (mother), 20

C
Camby, Marcus, 46
Campbell, Elden, 48, 66, 68
Charlotte Hornets, 46
Chicago Bulls, 57, 58, 62, 66, 74

D
Denver Nuggets, 63
Divac, Vlade, 46
Downer, Gregg, 25, 26, 30, 36
Drexler, Charles, 69
Duncan, Tim, 71
Dunleavy, Mike, 89

E
Egan, Michael, 32, 36
Erving, Julius, 19, 49, 51

F
fan club, 90
Fox, Rick, 66

G
Garnett, Kevin, 41
Golden State Warriors, 19, 76, 90

H
Hakeem Olajuwon, 69
Harper, Ron, 81
Harris, Del, 20, 55, 59, 67
Hatcher, Omar, 39
Hill, Grant, 7
Hill, Sonny, 25
Horry, Robert, 59, 82
Houston Rockets, 69–70

I
Indiana Pacers, 10–15, 83–84
Inside Sports, 61
Iverson, Allen, 46, 48, 78

J

Jackson, Phil, 9, 73, 74–75, 77, 79, 82, 90, 92
Jamison, Antawn, 90
Jennings, Jon, 41
Johnson, Earvin "Magic," 17, 23, 56, 73
Jones, Eddie, 48, 66, 68
Jordan, Michael, 7, 57–58, 61–62, 65

K

K.O.B.E., 88
Kerr, Steve, 75
Kersey, Jerome, 48
Kobe Klub, 90
Kobe's Reading Club, 88

L

LaSalle University, 19
Los Angeles Lakers
    1996 NBA draft, 44–48
    1996-97 season, 52–55
    1997-98 season, 57–64
    1998-99 season, 65–73
    1999-00 season, 9, 75–85
    2000-01 NBA Champions, 9–17, 90–92
    Dennis Rodman and, 67–69
Lower Merion High School, 25, 30, 33, 35–36

M

Malone, Karl, 53
Malone, Moses, 46
Miller, Reggie, 10, 13, 83
Minnesota Timberwolves, 76–77
Minor, Harold, 8
Monroe, Earl, 52

N

National Basketball Association (NBA), 83
Newsweek, 61

O

O'Neal, Shaquille, 13, 48, 64, 73, 78, 82–83, 85, 89–90
Orlando Magic, 48, 59, 68

P

Pangrazio, Dan, 32
Philadelphia 76ers, 19–20, 78, 92
Phoenix Suns, 9, 59, 79, 92
Pippen, Scottie, 10, 66, 69–70, 75, 81
Portland Trail Blazers, 9–10, 52, 63, 79–82, 92

R

Rambis, Kurt, 67, 68, 70
Rice, Glen, 15, 17, 68, 71, 90
Rider, Isaiah, 76, 89
Rieti, Italy, 21
Robinson, David, 70, 71
Rodman, Dennis, 66, 67–69

S

Sacramento Kings, 9, 78–79, 92
San Antonio Spurs, 70–73, 92
Scott, Byron, 48
Seattle SuperSonics, 61, 63
Shaw, Brian, 13, 82
Slam-Dunk Contest (1997), 48–52
Smits, Rick, 13
Sports Illustrated, 61
Stackhouse, Jerry, 7
Stern, David, 46
Stockton, John, 53

T

TeamUp Celebration, 88

U

Utah Jazz, 53, 55, 63

V

Van Exel, Nick, 48, 55–56, 66
Visions, 88

W

Wallace, Rasheed, 10, 63, 81
West, Jerry, 17, 43–44, 46, 61

Z

Zen Buddhism, 75